ALTERNATOR
BOOKS™

WEIRD PLANTS

Brianna Kaiser

Lerner Publications ◆ Minneapolis

Lerner Publications Company
An imprint of Lerner Publishing Group, Inc.
241 First Avenue North
Minneapolis, MN 55401 USA

For reading levels and more information, look up this title at www.lernerbooks.com.

Main body text set in Aptifer Sans LT Pro.
Typeface provided by Linotype AG.

Editor: Lauren Foley **Designer:** Mary Ross
Lerner team: Sue Marquis

Library of Congress Cataloging-in-Publication Data

Names: Kaiser, Brianna, 1996– author.
Title: Weird plants / Brianna Kaiser.
Description: Minneapolis : Lerner Publications, [2024] | Series: Wonderfully weird (Alternator books) | Includes bibliographical references and index. | Audience: Ages 8–12 | Audience: Grades 4–6 | Summary: "Have you ever seen a carnivorous plant? Plants are everywhere, but some are stranger than others. Journey from the tops of trees to under the sea to discover some of the most perplexing plants around"— Provided by publisher.
Identifiers: LCCN 2022033970 (print) | LCCN 2022033971 (ebook) | ISBN 9781728490724 (library binding) | ISBN 9798765601877 (ebook)
Subjects: LCSH: Plants—Juvenile literature.
Classification: LCC QK49 .K135 2024 (print) | LCC QK49 (ebook) | DDC 580—dc23/eng/20220721

LC record available at https://lccn.loc.gov/2022033970
LC ebook record available at https://lccn.loc.gov/2022033971

Manufactured in the United States of America
1-53003-51021-11/11/2022

TABLE OF CONTENTS

INTRODUCTION:
SNAPPING INTO ACTION

YOU ARE HIKING THROUGH THE FOREST WHEN YOU FIND A STRANGE-LOOKING PLANT. It has two lobes with hairlike spikes on their edges. Then you see an insect brush the spikes. Quickly, the lobes snap shut.

The Venus flytrap is a type of carnivorous plant native to North and South Carolina. These plants eat beetles, ants, spiders, and more. But they can go months between meals.

There are hundreds of thousands of plant species all around the world. Some, like the Venus flytrap, can seem more unusual than other kinds of plants. They can seem weird! From smelling bad to looking as though they are bleeding, plants can be weird in many kinds of ways.

CHAPTER 1:

TREES AROUND THE WORLD

SOME KINDS OF TREES CAN GROW ALL OVER THE WORLD. Others can only grow in specific places where their unique characteristics help them survive.

Socotra dragon trees have wide, domed tops.

SOCOTRA DRAGON TREE

The Socotra dragon tree has an odd umbrella shape. Its shape allows it to catch water from rain and mist. The tree gets its name from its red sap, or resin. This sap is called dragon's blood. For centuries, people have used the sap in art and in medicines.

The Socotra dragon tree grows on the island of Socotra, Yemen. And it isn't the only unusual plant on the island. Around 37 percent of the plant species on Socotra Island are not found anywhere else in the world.

PLANTS IN MEDICINE

People have used plants in medical practices for centuries to relieve pain and fight diseases. In India and China, the water hyssop, a tropical aquatic plant, has been used to support brain function. Researchers in New Delhi, India, are working to see if the water hyssop could help protect people's brains from declining as they get older.

A traveler's tree fanned out

TRAVELER'S TREE

A tree known as the traveler's tree, or traveler's palm, lives in Madagascar. The tree's trunk can grow more than 26 feet (8 m) tall. At the top of the trees are sets of leaves that look like a fan. Each leaf is about 13 to 16 feet (4 to 5 m) long.

The traveler's tree gathers water on the bases of its leaves. People may use the water for drinking in emergencies. Some people even use the tree as a compass because the fan of leaves usually grows on an east-west line.

Poland's Crooked Forest

Pine trees in the Crooked Forest outside Gryfino, Poland, bend outward at the base. And all the trees bend in the same direction! Why the trees grow this way remains a mystery.

RAINBOW EUCALYPTUS

One kind of eucalyptus tree, the rainbow eucalyptus, has trunks with stripes of neon colors. When the tree sheds its bark, a layer of neon colors appears. Some common colors are green, red, and orange.

The rainbow eucalyptus is the only kind of eucalyptus tree that is native to the Northern Hemisphere. It mainly grows in rainy, tropical forests in the Philippines, New Guinea, and Indonesia. Some rainbow eucalyptus trees are found in Hawaii, California, Texas, and Florida.

The trunk of a rainbow eucalyptus tree looks like a colorful work of art.

CHAPTER 2:
PLANTS THAT STINK AND KILL

PEOPLE OFTEN LOVE THE SMELL OF PLANTS AND FLOWERS, BUT SOME PLANTS REEK! Other plants even kill. Carnivorous plants eat insects and other animals. Both smelly and hungry plants can have strange effects on insects.

A blooming corpse flower

CORPSE FLOWER

The corpse flower is incredibly stinky. Many people think it smells like rotting flesh. The flower's smell is strongest during the night and into the early morning. Heat makes the smell travel farther, attracting insects such as beetles and flies from long distances.

The corpse flower is also large. It often grows up to 8 feet (2.4 m) tall. Many corpse flowers only bloom once every few years or longer. They only bloom when they have stored enough energy.

TROPICAL PITCHER PLANT

There are over a hundred species of tropical pitcher plants. They live in tropical habitats including India, Malaysia, and more. The soil in tropical habitats doesn't have many nutrients, so tropical pitcher plants get nutrients from eating insects and other prey.

Tropical pitcher plants have a lid, rim, and pitcher cup. The lid helps keep rainwater out. When it gets wet, the rim gets slippery. This makes it easier for insects to fall inside. The pitcher cup is shaped like a tube. Digestive fluids inside it break down prey.

A tropical pitcher plant

A Sensitive Plant

The Mimosa pudica is found in the tropics of Central and South America. The plant's leaves are covered with sensitive, tiny hairs. If something brushes these hairs, the plant folds up.

This blooming carrion flower will attract bugs like flies.

This blooming carrion flower will attract bugs like flies.

CARRION FLOWER

Carrion flowers are a type of succulent plant. Succulents have thick leaves or stems that store water. Carrion flowers live in tropical areas of southern Africa. They have four-sided grooved stems and can be purple, red, or yellow.

Although the flowers are beautiful, these plants have an unpleasant smell. People often describe it as smelling like rotting meat. The smell attracts flies. They lay their eggs in the flower and help pollinate it.

CHAPTER 3:

ODD LOOKS

SOME PLANTS ARE WEIRD BECAUSE THEY LOOK WEIRD. These plants may look different from other plants, or they may not even look like plants.

CREEPING DEVIL CACTUS

Can a creeping devil cactus walk? No, but it does move. The creeping devil cactus is the only moving cactus in the world. It moves or creeps through the desert over a long period. It grows horizontally from its stem and kills off its rear end. As it moves, it sprouts new roots to absorb water and nutrients.

Sometimes the creeping devil cactus grows in patches. Each cactus travels about 2 feet (0.6 m) every year. The creeping devil cactus is found in Baja California Sur in Mexico.

A patch of creeping devil cacti

p Growth

chia mirabilis of the Namib Desert leaves. The leaves grow during the f the plant. Some of the plants are hundred years old!

LITHOPS

Lithops are from southern Africa. They are small succulents, but they are often mistaken for stones because of their appearance. That is why they are sometimes called living stones. These plants have evolved to blend in with their surroundings. They often are the same shape, size, and color as nearby stones.

Lithops survive in arid regions, which get little rainfall, by storing water. They can live months without rain. Lithops often have two leaves with a narrow opening between them. There are dozens of species of Lithops, often different in shape, color, and texture.

Lithops can be many colors.

An adult *Hydnellum peckii* (*right*) doesn't push out sap like a young one (*left*).

HYDNELLUM PECKII

A young Hydnellum peckii looks very different from an adult. An adult mushroom is dull. But when it is young and growing, the white mushroom looks as though it is bleeding. People often call this mushroom the bleeding tooth fungus or the devil's tooth.

What looks like blood is a sap that is forced out of the mushroom when too much water gets into the roots. Hydnellum peckii are found in forests and mountainous areas in North America, Europe, Iran, and South Korea.

LIVING IN THE DARK

Many plants use photosynthesis to make food. During photosynthesis, plants capture energy from the sun to produce oxygen and energy as sugar. But the ghost plant doesn't use photosynthesis. These flowering plants use their root system to get nutrients from fungi. The ghost plant grows in dark environments. It is found in most of the US.

CHAPTER 4:
GROWING UP UNDERWATER

PLANTS AREN'T JUST FOUND ON LAND. A variety of
plants can be found in the ocean and in fresh water.
These plants do oddly amazing things.

KELP FORESTS

Similar to trees in a forest on land, kelp grows in groups. It grows in shallower waters close to shore along the Pacific coast of North America. Kelp is a brown kind of algae. It can grow up to 250 feet (76 m) long!

Kelp forests are home to more kinds of plants and animals than most other places in the ocean. Animals such as sea otters, whales, and gulls can be found there. Animals often use kelp forests for protection from predators or storms.

An underwater kelp forest off the coast of California

SEAGRASS

Seagrasses have long, grasslike leaves. These plants live in shallow, salty waters in many parts of the world, from the Arctic Circle to the tropics. There are over seventy species of seagrass.

Like kelp forests, seagrasses provide shelter and food for many kinds of animals, including turtles and crabs. Seagrasses can form underwater meadows. Some of the meadows are large enough to be seen from space!

Seagrass moving with the current in the Mediterranean Sea

Oxygen Sources

People need oxygen to live. Most of Earth's oxygen comes from the ocean. Marine plants and plankton produce about 50 to 80 percent of the oxygen made on Earth.

WATERWHEEL PLANT

The waterwheel plant is an aquatic Venus flytrap. Each plant has a group of about ten to fifteen flytraps, but some have up to two hundred traps! The entire plant is about 6 inches (15 cm) long. Just like the Venus flytrap, the waterwheel plant has trigger hairs on it. When small prey such as eelworms touch the trigger hairs, the waterwheel plant snaps shut, trapping the prey.

Waterwheel plants grow groups of traps in a wheel-like shape around their stem.

Waterwheel plants don't have roots. They float freely through the water. The only part of the plant that sits above the waterline is its one white flower. Waterwheel plants grow in ponds and lakes in Africa, Australia, India, Japan, and Europe.

MORE WEIRD PLANTS

So many kinds of weird plants live on Earth that it is impossible to list them all. And people may define weird in different ways. What plants do you think are weird? What do your friends think? Maybe you will make your own list or grow a garden of your own weird plants!

All kinds of habitats, such as this rain forest, might have weird plants.

GLOSSARY

aquatic: living or growing in the water

carnivorous: a kind of plant that gets some of its nutrients from eating insects and other animals

characteristic: a special quality of a plant

habitat: the natural environment of a plant

horizontally: being parallel to Earth's surface

native: a plant that originated in a place

pollinate: to transfer or carry pollen between plants to help make new ones grow

predator: an animal or plant that hunts other animals for food

prey: an animal that is hunted as food by another animal or plant

species: a group of living things that have similar characteristics

LEARN MORE

Britannica Kids: Water Plant
https://kids.britannica.com/students/article/water-plant/277674

Golusky, Jackie. *Weird Places*. Minneapolis: Lerner Publications, 2024.

Griffin, Mary. *Kelp Forests*. New York: PowerKids, 2023.

Hirsch, Rebecca E. *When Plants Attack: Strange and Terrifying Plants*. Minneapolis: Millbrook Press, 2019.

Markovics, Joyce L. *Poisonous Plants*. Ann Arbor, MI: Cherry Lake, 2021.

National Geographic Kids: Awesome 8 Carnivorous Plants
https://kids.nationalgeographic.com/awesome-8/article/carnivorous-plants

National Geographic Kids: Habitats
https://kids.nationalgeographic.com/nature/habitats

Plants for Kids
https://easyscienceforkids.com/plants-for-kids-video/

INDEX

PHOTO ACKNOWLEDGMENTS

Image credits: Oli Anderson/Getty Images, pp. 4–5; Photography by P. Lubas/Getty Images, p. 6; Csilla Zelko/Getty Images, p. 7; dr322/Getty Images, p. 9; A. Michael Brown/Shutterstock, pp. 10–11; Jenny Dettrick/Getty Images, p. 12; Rhododendrites/Wikimedia Commons (CC BY-SA 4.0), p. 13; Photography by Mangiwau/Getty Images, p. 14; Deidre Booy/Getty Images, p. 15; iwciagr/Shutterstock, pp. 16, 20; Darrel Guilbeau/Shutterstock, p. 17; SIM ONE/Shutterstock, pp. 18–19; Svitlyk/Shutterstock, p. 20; Andrew b Stowe/Shutterstock, p. 22; Douglas Klug/Getty Images, p. 23; Pommeyrol Vincent/Shutterstock, pp. 24–25; Paul Starosta/Getty Images, pp. 26–27; Ghislain & Marie David de Lossy/Getty Images, pp. 28–29.
Cover: Fadil Aziz/Getty Images.